FIGHTER PILOT

by Bill Holder

Willowisp
Press®

To the 178th Tactical Fighter Group,
Air National Guard, Springfield, Ohio

photos by John Farquhar
and the Department of Defense Stillmedia

Published by Willowisp Press, Inc.
401 E. Wilson Bridge Road, Worthington, Ohio 43085

Printed in the United States of America

10 9 8 7 6 5 4 3 2 1

ISBN 0-87406-470-8

CONTENTS

IN THE AIR AGAIN

Everything checks out A-OK. You're strapped into the cockpit. Your G-suit is working perfectly. The custom-fitted helmet, with your radio and oxygen supply, is on. The ground crew checks out your engine.

When you're ready, the crew chief waves you out. On the runway, you wait for the final go-ahead. You press the brakes down as hard as you can and rev your engine up to full power. You get the final A-OK and you're ready to roll!

Then it's brakes off, and you start down the runway. You begin to pick up speed. The needle on your air speed indicator reaches upward. You feel the force of your acceleration press against you.

When your speed reaches 185 miles per hour, you know it's time to get this bird into the air. You raise the plane's nose and then you experience the greatest thrill you've ever known. You'll never get tired of it as long as you live.

You're in the air again!

Have you ever wondered what it's like to be the pilot of a jet fighter? This book will put you in the cockpit. You'll hear the roar of your mighty turbojet engine as it cranks out 12,000 pounds of thrust. You'll see the awesome control panel spread out before you, with all its needles, dials, and gages. You'll thrill to the sight of the ground falling far below as you climb higher into the sky. And you'll feel the tremendous power surge as you push the throttle to full power and get closer to your top speed of 690 miles per hour.

THE A-7D CORSAIR II

Your airplane has one of the most famous names in military aircraft history. There was a biplane in the 1920s called a Corsair. And in World War II, another plane called the Corsair fought many battles in the Pacific. Your plane, the Corsair II, was born when the U.S. Navy needed a new plane that could carry a heavy bomb load and operate off of aircraft carriers. The A-7 saw its first action in 1965 in the Vietnam War.

Other versions of the Corsair II were built for the U.S. Air Force. These were called A-7Ds, and they're still going strong today. During the 1970s, the Air Force transferred the Corsair IIs to the Air National Guard. Crews all over the country keep the Corsair II combat-ready.

Let's take a closer look at the A-7D. It has what's called a high-wing design. That means that its wings are mounted on the top of its body. The wings are swept back for greater speeds. They can also be folded up, so that the plane can be easily parked on aircraft carriers. There's a bubble on the front of the body that houses radar equipment. It's called the radome. Under the radome is a 20-millimeter machine gun called a Gatling gun. The Corsair II can also carry Sidewinder air-to-air missiles.

A fully loaded Corsair II weighs 33,000 pounds—as much as 12 cars. Maximum speed for this jet is 690 miles per hour. That's not very fast compared to jets of the 1980s such as the F-15 Eagle and the F-14 Tomcat. But the Corsair II was designed to fly far with a heavy load of bombs, missiles, and fuel. And it can do that. With its 2,700 gallons of fuel, the jet has a range of about 2,900 miles. That means it can fly from New York to California without refueling!

FLIGHT TRAINING

You don't just sit down in the cockpit of a jet aircraft and take off—no way! All the training you'll need adds up to almost two solid years. You begin at the Air Force flight school, which takes about a year. USAF flight school is no piece of cake! There's tons of bookwork, in addition to the actual flying practice. A lot of people apply, but only a few make it to flight school.

If you're one of the tough ones, the lucky ones, you go from flight school to what is called Lead-In training for 12 weeks. But school's not over yet. Next is the six-month A-7 pilot school in Tucson, Arizona. After all, a jet fighter costs an awful lot of money, and the Air Force wants only the best pilots sitting in its seat.

But if you're tough, and study hard, you'll make it. How proud do you think a guy feels when his commanding officer finally presents him with those silver wings that tell the world he's a real pilot?

IN ACTION

The Corsair II is called a fighter-bomber. It was designed to do both these jobs. The *A* in its name stands for *Attack,* and that's just what it can do best. The plane's name, Corsair, is another name for a pirate. You can bet the sight of an A-7D screaming out of the sun is just as unpleasant a sight to an enemy fighter as the old skull and crossbones Jolly Roger flag was on the high seas!

The Corsair II performs two missions very well. The first is called air-to-ground, or bombing. Pilots usually don't use real bombs when they're practicing. The small, blue bombs used in practice weigh 25 pounds and have smoke charges inside. This way, the pilot can tell how close he's come to hitting the target.

The second mission, the air-to-air, is a fight between planes in the sky. It's sometimes called a dogfight. The planes use their weapons to try to down the enemy. To practice air-to-air missions, A-7D pilots compete against other planes and pilots. It's sort of like a game. But every fighter pilot knows that the training in outsmarting, outthinking, and outflying the other guy could someday turn into the real thing.

WEAPONS

The Corsair II's 20mm Gatling machine gun can fire an incredible 6,000 rounds, or individual bullets, a minute. But pilots never fire the gun for more than a few seconds, to avoid damage to the gun barrels. The plane only carries 1,000 rounds, so pilots have to be careful how they use the ammunition. They fire it in short bursts of about 50-100 rounds.

The A-7D also carries Sidewinder missiles in two places on the sides of its body. The Sidewinder is a heat-seeking missile, which actually locks onto the heat coming from the target.

The pilot just moves in behind the enemy fighter and fires the missile. The Sidewinder does the rest!

The Corsair II can carry a pretty amazing assortment of weapons, weighing up to seven and a half tons. That's like asking a fairly little plane to take off with four small cars hanging on it!

The plane can carry 3,500 pounds of bombs on each wing and another 2,500 pounds on each inner wing point, for a total of 12,000 pounds of bombs. It can also be fitted to carry rocket launchers, missiles, flares, and electronic pods for various uses. You might think the plane would have a tough time getting off the ground with all that equipment. But that's what the Corsair II was designed to do!

COMING IN FOR A LANDING

It's time to bring your A-7D in for a landing! You're approaching the runway at about 1,500 feet altitude. You peal off in a hard turn and cut back the engine power, which slows your speed to about 250 mph. You lower your landing gear and wing flaps.

You touch down with the plane's nose up. You cruise down the runway with the nose wheel off the ground to slow the plane. Your plane finally slows down enough so that the nose wheel settles onto the ground. You usually try to use the whole runway because this saves your plane's brakes.

MIDAIR REFUELING

Even though your Corsair II can carry 2,700 gallons of jet fuel, you sometimes need to refuel in flight. But you're not worried—you've practiced midair refueling at least six times a year. Still, it's a pretty tricky operation. Let a real A-7D pilot explain how it's done.

"You fly your plane up to the KC-10 or KC-135 jet tanker from behind and below. Then the refueling boom is pushed out toward you by the operator in the back of the tanker. The operator actually flies the boom out to your plane with the small wings that are on the boom. The boom makes a 'thunk' when it's hooked up to your plane. When your tank is filled up, the boom will be pulled out. You cut back the engine power and fall away from the tanker."

BAILING OUT

But what if there's an emergency and you have to bail out? It may only happen in one in a million flights, but you have to be ready—just in case. Many times, you'll be able to start up your engine again. But if you can't, the first thing you do is get your plane pointed away from towns or cities. You have to be at least a half-mile up so that your parachute will have time to open. You slow down the plane as much as you can.

Then, when it's time to "punch out," you pull the handle in your seat. The canopy is blown away. Then a rocket motor drives the seat, with you still in it, about a hundred feet straight up. It all happens really fast. The next thing you know, your chute's opened and you're floating back to earth! You're glad the people who packed your parachute knew what they were doing!

PART OF A TEAM

Flying an airplane takes a lot of people working together. You, the pilot, are just one of many people doing the same job—keeping the Corsair II in the air. You wouldn't be where you are, screaming through the skies at 600 miles an hour, without your teammates.

Your crew chief and mechanics know the plane inside and out. They've been working on it for years, performing regular checkups, inspections, and maintenance. If there's a problem with your A-7D, the talented men and women on your crew are going to find it! After every 200 hours of flying time, your plane is brought into the hangar for a complete check. And every 1,200 hours, the plane goes back to the service depot.

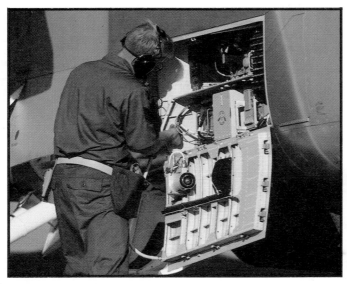

LIVING THE DREAM

Here you are. You've worked and worked to get here. Now you're the one in the pilot's seat, with your hand on the control stick and your eye on the instrument panel. Sure, you've got a job to do, just like anyone else.

But you know that this job isn't like any other. Nothing else compares with the feeling of screaming across the sky, riding a hot, metal monster at incredible speeds.

You're living a life that other people only dream about. You're a jet fighter pilot.

GLOSSARY

air-speed indicator A gage that tells the pilot how fast his plane is flying.

canopy The clear, ultra-hard plastic covering over the cockpit.

cockpit The place on top of the plane's body where the pilot sits.

crew chief The head of the crew, who's responsible for making sure that everything is A-OK on the pilot's A-7D.

Gatling gun The machine gun on many jet fighters. Early forms of the Gatling gun were used in the American Civil War.

G-suit The protective suit worn by a jet fighter pilot to protect him from the dangerous effects of quick acceleration.

hangar A large building where airplanes are stored and repaired.

heat-seeking missile A missile that locks onto a heat source and destroys it. The Sidewinder is a heat-seeking missile.

radome A large, plastic cone on the front of the plane that houses the radar equipment. A shortened form of *radar dome*.

range The distance a plane can travel on one load of fuel.

thrust The pushing force of an engine.

INDEX